Pebble®
Plus

Look Inside

Look Inside a Pyramid

by Mari Schuh

Consulting Editor: Gail Saunders-Smith, PhD

Consultant: Leo Depuydt, Professor
Department of Egyptology and Ancient Western Asian Studies
Brown University
Providence, Rhode Island

Capstone
press

Mankato, Minnesota

Pebble Plus is published by Capstone Press,
151 Good Counsel Drive, P.O. Box 669, Mankato, Minnesota 56002.
www.capstonepress.com

1 2 3 4 5 6 14 13 12 11 10 09

Library of Congress Cataloging-in-Publication Data
Schuh, Mari C., 1975–
    Look inside a pyramid / by Mari Schuh.
    p. cm. — (Pebble plus. Look inside)
    Includes bibliographical references and index.
    Summary: "Simple text and photographs present ancient Egyptian pyramids, their construction, and their
interaction with the environment" — Provided by publisher.
    ISBN-13: 978-1-4296-2247-9 (hardcover)
    ISBN-10: 1-4296-2247-4 (hardcover)
    1. Pyramids — Egypt — Juvenile literature. I. Title.
DT63.S35 2009
932 — dc22   2008027652

Editorial Credits
Megan Peterson, editor; Renée T. Doyle, designer; Wanda Winch, photo researcher

Photo Credits
Capstone Press/Renée Doyle, sun graphic by page numbers, 24
Corbis/epa/Handout/Dassault Systemes, 13
Dorking Kindersley/Maltings Partnership, 17; Richard Bonson, 9
iStockphoto/Ian Stewart, 15; Ryka Witold, 19
Jupiterimages Corporation, 16
Peter Arnold/Fotoagentur imo- ullstein, 21
Shutterstock/Adrian Lindley, 1, 22–23; nagib, back cover, 3; sculpies, front cover; Vladimir Korostyshevskiy, 5
Wood Ronsaville Harlin, Inc./Greg Harlin, 11; Rob Wood, 7

Note to Parents and Teachers

The Look Inside set supports national social studies standards related to people, places, and culture. This book describes and illustrates ancient Egyptian pyramids. The images support early readers in understanding the text. The repetition of words and phrases helps early readers learn new words. This book also introduces early readers to subject-specific vocabulary words, which are defined in the Glossary section. Early readers may need assistance to read some words and to use the Table of Contents, Glossary, Read More, Internet Sites, and Index sections of the book.

Table of Contents

What Is a Pyramid?

A pyramid is a big tomb.

Pyramids were built in Egypt

long ago.

Kings were buried

in pyramids.

Building a Pyramid

To build a pyramid,

workers used limestone

and granite.

They cut the heavy stone

out of the ground.

Boats carried the stone.

The boats floated

down the Nile River

to the work site.

Workers pushed the stone

onto logs or sleds.

They pulled the sleds

up ramps that wrapped

around the pyramid.

Workers stacked the stone

one by one for many years.

The tallest pyramid grew to be

481 feet (147 meters) high.

Workers added white stone
to the outside of the pyramid.
They rubbed the stone
to make it shine.

remaining white stone

Inside a Pyramid

A small door let people inside the pyramid. Tunnels led to rooms filled with the king's treasures.

door

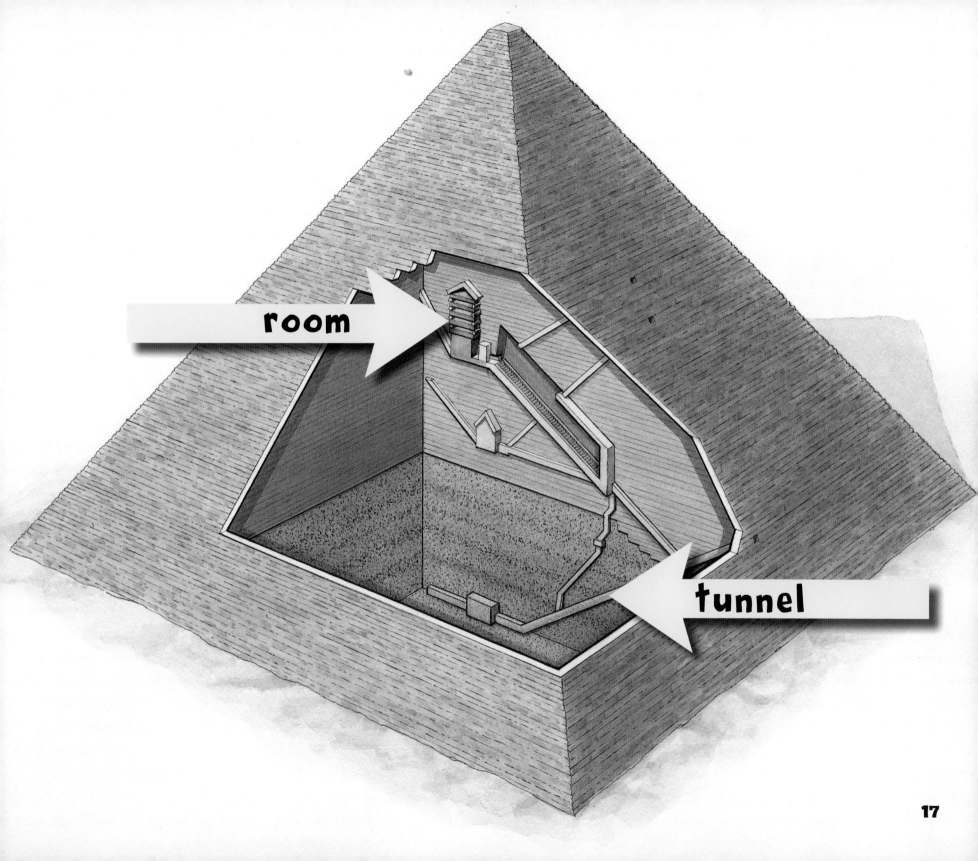

room

tunnel

The king was buried

in his own room.

Writing covered the walls

in some pyramids.

Pyramids Today

Today people from
around the world
visit Egypt's pyramids.
Pyramids show us how people
in Egypt lived long ago.

Glossary

granite — a hard rock used in building

king — a man from a royal family who is ruler of his country; in Egypt, kings were also called pharaohs.

limestone — a hard rock used in building

pyramid — a very old stone monument in Egypt; each of the four sides of a pyramid is shaped like a triangle.

ramp — a surface that slants to join two levels; people believe that workers in Egypt used ramps to build the pyramids.

tomb — a room or building that holds a dead body

treasure — gold, jewels, money, statues, or other valuable items that have been hidden; workers hid treasures inside the pyramids.

tunnel — a narrow passageway

Read More

Rau, Dana Meachen. *Pyramid.* The Inside Story. New York: Marshall Cavendish Benchmark, 2007.

Spengler, Kremena. *Pyramids.* Ancient Egypt. Mankato, Minn.: Capstone Press, 2009.

Internet Sites

FactHound offers a safe, fun way to find educator-approved Internet sites related to this book.

Here's what you do:

1. Visit *www.facthound.com*
2. Choose your grade level.
3. Begin your search.

This book's ID number is 9781429622479.

FactHound will fetch the best sites for you!

Index

Word Count: 160
Grade: 1
Early-Intervention Level: 18